W9-DAE-509

Cuban
Americans

Dale Anderson

Curriculum Consultant: Michael Koren,
Social Studies Teacher, Maple Dale School, Fox Point, Wisconsin

WORLD ALMANAC® LIBRARY

A los Padrinos, sobre todo a Mercedes, con mucha admiración por su fuerza, profunda gratitud, y muchísimo cariño.

Please visit our web site at: www.garethstevens.com
For a free color catalog describing World Almanac® Library's list of high-quality books and multimedia programs, call 1-800-848-2928 (USA) or 1-800-387-3178 (Canada). World Almanac® Library's fax: (414) 332-3567.

Library of Congress Cataloging-in-Publication Data

Anderson, Dale, 1953-
    Cuban Americans / by Dale Anderson.
       p. cm. – (World Almanac Library of American immigration)
    Includes bibliographical references and index.
    ISBN-10: 0-8368-7309-2 – ISBN-13: 978-0-8368-7309-2 (lib. bdg.)
    ISBN-10: 0-8368-7322-X – ISBN-13: 978-0-8368-7322-1 (softcover)
    1. Cuban Americans–History–Juvenile literature. 2. Cuban Americans–Social conditions–Juvenile literature. 3. Immigrants–United States–History–Juvenile literature. 4. Cuba–Emigration and immigration–History–Juvenile literature. 5. United States–Emigration and immigration–History–Juvenile literature. I. Title. II. Series.
    E184.C97A54   2007
    973'.004687291–dc22   2006005642

First published in 2007 by
World Almanac® Library
A member of the WRC Media Family of Companies
330 West Olive Street, Suite 100
Milwaukee, WI 53212, USA

Copyright © 2007 by World Almanac® Library.

Produced by Discovery Books
Editor: Sabrina Crewe
Designer and page production: Sabine Beaupré
Photo researcher: Sabrina Crewe
Maps and diagrams: Stefan Chabluk
Consultant: Raúl C. Galván
Gareth Stevens editorial direction: Mark J. Sachner
Gareth Stevens editor: Barbara Kiely Miller
Gareth Stevens art direction: Tammy West
Gareth Stevens production: Jessica Morris

Picture credits: Dale Anderson: 30 (both); CORBIS: 11, 18, 43; Cuban Heritage Collection, University of Miami Libraries: 6, 15, 33, 36; Getty Images: 29; Historical Museum of Southern Florida: 41; John Fitzgerald Kennedy Library: 10; Library of Congress: 7, 12, 27, 28; State Archives of Florida: cover, title page, 5, 8, 17, 20, 22, 23, 24, 25, 26, 35, 39, 42; United States Coast Guard: 19.

Printed in the United States of America

1 2 3 4 5 6 7 8 9 10 09 08 07 06

Contents

Front cover: The *comparsa* dance was introduced in the United States by Cuban Americans in the 1930s. Like many Cuban traditions, the dance combines African and Spanish influences. This photograph shows the Cayo Hueso Comparsa Dancers in Key West, Florida.

Title page: During the 1960s and 1970s, many thousands of Cubans sought refuge in the United States. They came by airplane or in small boats, such as this one that arrived in Miami, Florida, in 1962.

 # Introduction

T he United States has often been called "a nation of immigrants." With the exception of Native Americans— who have inhabited North America for thousands of years— all Americans can trace their roots to other parts of the world.

Immigration is not a thing of the past. More than seventy million people came to the United States between 1820 and 2005. One-fifth of that total—about fourteen million people— immigrated since the start of 1990. Overall, more people have immigrated permanently to the United States than to any other single nation.

Push and Pull

Historians write of the "push" and "pull" factors that lead people to emigrate. "Push" factors are the conditions in the homeland that convince people to leave. Many immigrants to the United States were—and still are—fleeing persecution or poverty. "Pull" factors are those that attract people to settle in another country. The dream of freedom or jobs or both continues to pull immigrants to the United States. People from many countries around the world view the United States as a place of opportunity.

Building a Nation

Immigrants to the United States have not always found what they expected. People worked long hours for little pay, often doing jobs that others did not want to do. Many groups also endured prejudice.

In spite of these challenges, immigrants and their children built the United States of America, from its farms, railroads, and com- puter industries to its beliefs and traditions. They have enriched American life with their culture and ideas. Although they honor their heritage, most immigrants and their descendants are proud to call themselves Americans first and foremost.

> "I am always thankful for the choice [my parents] made [to come to the United States] even though it was very hard on them. My family is mostly in the United States; however, we still have some back in Cuba and we try to help them the best we can. There is an enormous guilt every time I examine my life and theirs."
>
> *Marisel Sanchez Walston, who came to the United States from Cuba in 1979*

▲ Cuban Americans have brought their history and culture with them to the United States. These men sing *décimas*, ten-line verses they compose themselves. Décimas are a traditional part of Cuban folk music.

Coming from Cuba

Cuba, a small island in the Caribbean Sea, lies only 90 miles (145 kilometers) south of Florida. Being so close to the United States has influenced Cuba's history. The closeness has also played a major part in the immigration of Cubans to the United States.

The first group of Cubans to come to the United States, just a few thousand people, came in stages before 1890. The next group trickled in over the years to 1960. Political changes in Cuba launched the next wave—the exodus of more than 470,000 people from Cuba to the United States in the 1960s and 1970s. Between 1980 and 2005, almost 400,000 more Cubans arrived.

Cuban Americans

In the United States, Cuban Americans are considered Hispanics, or Latinos. They share the Spanish language and some Spanish traditions with other people from the Caribbean and Central and South America. Each Latino group, however, has a special character born of its own history and culture. Many Cuban Americans left Cuba for political reasons and consider themselves exiles. This view has profoundly shaped their lives in the United States. Cuban Americans also have a clear idea of their uniqueness and an intense pride in both their homeland and their achievements in the United States.

CHAPTER 1

Life in the Homeland

Cuba was one of the first parts of the Americas to come under Spanish rule in the 1500s. The fertile land and warm climate created ideal conditions for growing tobacco, coffee, and sugar, and these products made Cuba a valued colony.

Cuban Society

Cuban culture blends Spanish, African, and North American influences. Spanish colonial rule brought Spanish law, cooking, language, literature, and the Roman Catholic religion to Cuba. African rhythms, originally introduced by Africans brought to the island as slaves, form the beat underlying today's Cuban music. African influence also appears in the practice of *santería*,

▼ As a colony of Spain, the island of Cuba was a major sugar producer. A postcard from the early 1900s shows Cuban workers filling a cart with sugarcane.

▶ Black Cubans did not usually have an equal place in Cuban society, but Antonio Maceo (1848–1896) became a hero to all Cubans. He was an outstanding leader who died fighting for Cuban independence.

a religious tradition that combines the Orisha religion of the Yoruba people from Africa with Roman Catholic beliefs. Black Cubans, the descendants of slaves, did not enjoy full equality even after slavery was abolished in Cuba in 1886. They had the worst, lowest paying jobs and lived in the poorest conditions.

In traditional Cuban families, life centered on the nuclear family of parents and children. Children were expected to follow their parents' wishes and obey their instructions. Fathers generally dominated family decisions, but many mothers managed to shape these decisions. Families were often large, especially in rural areas. Adult children tended to live near their parents, to whom they showed great love and respect.

Fighting for Independence

Creoles—people of Spanish descent born in Cuba—resented the fact that Spanish-born people controlled the government. In 1868, a wealthy Creole landowner launched a revolt that started the Ten

The People of Cuba

Cuba's population—just over eleven million people in 2005—is made up primarily of three groups. About one-third of the people are of European ancestry. Most of this group are Creoles, people descended from Spanish colonists. About 10 percent of the population is black, the descendants of African slaves. The largest group, comprising just over half the people, has mixed white and black ancestry. A tiny number of Cubans—between three and five thousand—are Chinese. A very small number of people trace their families to Cuban Indians, but the vast majority of these native people of Cuba died out soon after the Spanish arrived because of disease and harsh treatment.

These Cuban Americans from Jacksonville and Key West, Florida, and from New York City were among the exiles who formed the Army of the Cuban Republic. They sailed to Cuba in 1898 to join the fight against Spain.

Years' War, a conflict that lasted until 1878. Spain ended the war by promising changes to the way it governed Cuba.

> "I am in daily danger of giving my life for my country and duty for I understand that duty and have the courage to carry it out."
>
> *José Martí, letter to Mexican friend, May 18, 1895*

Some Cubans who supported independence were sent into exile by the Spanish and left for the United States. Between 1870 and 1900, a few other Cubans decided to emigrate because of poverty at home, hoping to find work in the United States.

Back in Cuba, meanwhile, the Spanish did not make the promised reforms. Political leaders living in exile in the United States, such as José Martí and Antonio Maceo, kept the idea of independence alive. In 1895, they launched a new war for independence.

The United States—Influence and Intervention

U.S. influence on Cuba, meanwhile, grew in the late 1800s and throughout the 1900s. As early as the 1870s, the American game of baseball became popular in Cuba. Protestant faiths attracted people because they reflected U.S. culture, which appealed to many Cubans. Christian Cubans celebrated Christmas Day, like North Americans, along with Three King's Day, like Spaniards. Cubans also adopted holidays such as Mother's Day and Valentine's Day.

In the United States, some Americans supported Cuban independence for the sake of freedom. Others, including some Cuban Americans, hoped the United States would seize the island once Spain was defeated. In 1898, the United States declared war on Spain, and the Spanish-American War began. The United States sent ships and troops to Cuba, and, when Spain surrendered a few months later, U.S. troops remained on the island. They maintained control there for several years, but in 1901 Cubans formed a government for the new Republic of Cuba and wrote a constitution. The Platt Amendment to the constitution, however, allowed the United States to land troops on the island whenever it chose to.

▲ This map shows how close Cuba lies to the U.S. state of Florida. Fidel Castro wanted to end U.S. domination of the Cuban economy and cut the island off from U.S. influence and ideas.

The Cuban Republic

For several decades, Cuba was governed sometimes by dictators and sometimes by elected leaders bent on reform. Through the early 1900s, Cuba's economy expanded, but that expansion carried problems. The country relied on sugar exports to the United States, but U.S. companies gained control of the sugar industry. U.S. businesses also flooded Cuba with their cheap products and blocked Cuban industries from developing.

During this period, a variety of reasons caused Cubans to emigrate to the United States. Some decided to leave for political reasons, such as opposition to someone who was in power at the time. Others went looking for work and to escape poverty and other social problems. Still others went abroad to study and then returned home.

Castro Takes Control

By 1958, the corrupt government of Cuban ruler Fulgencio Batista had controlled Cuba for many years. Batista's rule had become brutal, and he was losing the support of the people, the army, and the United States. A young lawyer named Fidel Castro, meanwhile, had built up support and recruited a force of about seven thousand men. In 1958, Castro's forces began moving across the island. The night of December 31, 1958, Batista fled Cuba, and Castro took control.

Very quickly, Castro began a social revolution. His communist government issued a land reform law that carved up large land-holdings into parcels for the poor. The law ended domination by U.S. companies, but it also destroyed Cuban-owned family farms. Castro postponed new elections. In 1960, he closed several newspapers that criticized him and seized the country's main television station.

Relations Between Cuba and the United States

Cuban relations with the United States soured when Castro came to power. In 1960, the U.S. government banned the purchase of Cuban sugar, and the next year it cut off diplomatic relations with Cuba. Relations remain broken today.

When John F. Kennedy became president, he approved a plan to land a force of Cuban exiles in Cuba to begin a revolt against Castro. On April 17, 1961, the small force landed at the Bay of Pigs, but it was poorly prepared and supported. The fighters were trapped and captured. Soon after, Kennedy ordered an embargo, blocking the sale of U.S. goods to Cuba.

Cuba, meanwhile, formed ties with the communist Soviet Union. In 1962, U.S. spy planes found that Soviet nuclear missiles were being placed on the island. Kennedy threatened military action if the missiles were not removed. For a few days—a period known as the Cuban Missile Crisis—the world waited, in fear of nuclear war. To settle the crisis, the Soviets agreed to remove the missiles, while Kennedy promised that the United States would not invade Cuba.

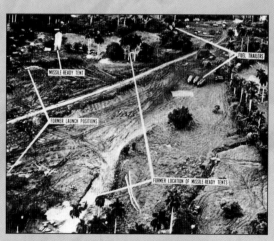

▲ A 1962 photograph, taken a few days after the Cuban Missile Crisis ended, shows one of the Soviet missile launch sites in Cuba that prompted the crisis.

The 1962 trade embargo ordered by President Kennedy remains in effect, with some changes. In 1992, a new law loosened the limits to allow medicine to be sold to Cuba; later, food shipments were permitted as well. Cuban Americans are divided about the embargo. Many support it, hoping that the economic pressure on Castro will produce events that force him from power. Others think the embargo should be ended. They say it contributes to poor relations between Cuba and the United States and thus helps Castro retain his grip on Cuba.

▲ In March 2005, relatives of jailed dissidents gathered on church steps in Havana, Cuba, quietly protesting the imprisonment of husbands, fathers, and sons.

Changing the Cuban Economy and Society

Castro radically changed Cuba's economy and society. Plans to cut the country's reliance on the sugar industry created a disaster, because no other parts of the economy grew to take its place. When food shortages appeared, the government began to ration food.

Castro launched a massive literacy campaign in 1961 aimed at teaching rural dwellers to read. The government also formed the Cuban Pioneers' Union to teach revolutionary ideals to children.

In 1960, the government set up groups named the Committees in the Defense of the Revolution. The groups recruited volunteers willing to report people who acted or made statements against the revolution. Neighbor spied on neighbor. Before long, there were thousands of Cubans wanting to leave their homeland.

The Revolution Today

Cuba's fragile economy has changed over the years. For decades, the Cuban economy was supported in part by money from the Soviet Union, a large communist power. Cuba lost this support, however, after the Soviet Union disbanded in 1991. More recently, the nation has received financial help from Venezuela.

The Cuban government has developed its tourist industry with new hotels and resorts that welcome about two million tourists a year. Outside tourist areas, however, problems abound. Cuba's well-regarded health care system suffers from a lack of supplies. Housing stock has deteriorated because new buildings were not constructed, and food is still in short supply. Repression has continued as well, with the government frequently arresting dissidents. Some or all of these problems continue to convince Cubans to leave their country.

CHAPTER 2

Emigration

T wo primary "push" factors have convinced people to leave Cuba—economic hardship and political worries. The United States has attracted Cubans because it is close by and can provide jobs and political refuge.

Emigration Before 1960

Some of those who left Cuba before 1890 were exiled by Spanish officials for taking part in the independence movement. Many, like José Martí, did not come directly to the United States but went first to another country. Other Cubans who emigrated before 1890 were looking for jobs. They settled in Key West or Tampa, Florida, to join the growing cigar industries in those cities. A smaller number of Cubans came to the United States as students.

Sailing ships and steamships regularly plied the narrow strait between Cuba and Florida. Passage was cheap and convenient, and ships made the crossing in just a day. Between 1901 and 1960, about two hundred thousand Cubans came to the United States. After earning money—or attending school—the majority returned home. As a result, fewer than eighty thousand Cubans lived in the United States in 1960. Castro's revolution quickly changed those numbers.

◄ One of the earliest Cuban exiles, José Martí (1853–1895) is revered by Cubans for his beautiful poetry and for his leadership in the cause of independence. In 1895, he left New York to renew the fight in Cuba, where he died in battle shortly after landing on the island.

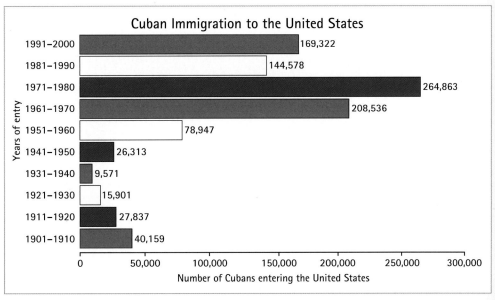

Cuban Immigration to the United States

Years of entry	Number of Cubans entering the United States
1991–2000	169,322
1981–1990	144,578
1971–1980	264,863
1961–1970	208,536
1951–1960	78,947
1941–1950	26,313
1931–1940	9,571
1921–1930	15,901
1911–1920	27,837
1901–1910	40,159

Source: U.S. Citizenship and Immigration Services, 1901–2000

▲ This chart shows how many people came from Cuba to the United States between 1901 and 2000. The numbers jumped dramatically in the 1960s and 1970s.

The Exodus Begins

Many of those who left Cuba in the first years of Castro's rule were Batista supporters who feared for their lives. Others were professionals—doctors, lawyers, or engineers—who mistrusted Castro and his speeches about a new society. These first emigrants in the 1960s expected that they would return to Cuba when Castro was removed from power.

Large numbers of Cubans went to the U.S. embassy in Havana to ask for visa waivers, the papers that would allow them to enter without visas. Demand for these waivers was high—the embassy received as many as twelve hundred requests each day in late 1961.

To leave Cuba, emigrants also had to gain permission from Castro's government. Starting in late 1961, the Cuban government made it more difficult for anyone to leave. Those who wanted to emigrate had to fill out many forms, pay fees in U.S. dollars, and wait long periods of time. Families had to leave all their possessions behind—furniture, valuables, and even items of sentimental value. People were allowed to take only $5 (about $30 today) and 30 pounds (14 kilograms) of luggage.

From 1962 to 1965

In addition to making it hard for Cubans to leave, Castro's government officials began referring to emigrants as *gusanos,* or worms,

Operation Pedro Pan

Many middle-class and upper middle-class parents resented the changes Castro made to the nation's schools. A group of Cubans and an American educator in Cuba made contact with a priest in Florida. Together, they launched an effort that came to be called "Operation Pedro Pan." Late in 1960, the first Pedro Pan flight took Cuban children to the United States. Between April 1961 and October 1962, the program helped more than fourteen thousand Cuban children emigrate to the United States. Their parents remained behind. The program ended abruptly in 1962, with the Cuban Missile Crisis.

"When you left the country after '60, you could not leave anything to anybody. You are supposed to turn everything [over] to the government. The moment you submit the papers, you're not supposed to get anything out of the house. . . . And that was the end of it. You lose everything. Whatever was inside, it's the government's property."

Roberto Ortiz, who came to the United States from Cuba in 1962

and traitors. During the Cuban Missile Crisis of October 1962, Castro stopped all flights to the United States.

For the next three years, nearly fifty-six thousand Cubans left the island for the United States by going through Spain, Mexico, or other countries. Those with family members already in the United States were given special priority by U.S. officials. Some bold Cubans came directly by sea, sailing on boats they had secretly bought or built themselves. About four thousand Cubans came this way in 1962 and 1963 alone.

Freedom Flights

Since the U.S. government used these boat journeys as propaganda against Castro's rule, Castro tried to turn the situation around. On September 28, 1965, he announced that Cubans with family in the United States were free to leave the country. Castro expected that the United States would not accept a new influx of refugees. President Lyndon Johnson, however, said that the Cubans would be welcomed.

On December 1, 1965, the "Freedom Flights" began. Until April 6, 1973, three to four thousand Cubans flew to the United States each month on one of two daily flights. By the time Castro halted

▶ An eight-year-old Cuban girl was photographed the day she left her home in Cuba during the Freedom Flights of 1965 to 1973. People had to leave most of their possessions behind, so anything they brought with them was precious.

the flights in 1973, the planes had carried almost three hundred thousand people to the United States.

Not everyone wanting to leave could do so—the Cuban government blocked the departure of doctors and those with technical skills. Teenage boys had to stay to serve in the military. The government harassed those it did allow to leave. At the airport, police officers inspected each person. They seized people's jewelry, including everything from wedding rings to young girls' earrings.

The New Emigrants

The people who emigrated on the Freedom Flights differed from the first exiles who came from 1959 to 1962. Up to 1962, more than 30 percent of those leaving Cuba had worked as professionals or managers. During the Freedom Flights, these groups made up only about 10 percent. More than half of the new emigrants had worked in factories or on farms. Others were women joining their husbands or older people going to live with adult children.

About half of all Chinese Cubans—a few thousand—left in the Freedom Flights. Many of these people had owned businesses in Cuba. They suffered in 1968 when Castro's government took control of thousands of stores and restaurants across the island.

> "At the airport, the [state police] made us disrobe, and they checked all our personal belongings. Everybody . . . even babies in diapers . . . even old people. They were so arrogant. . . . But we didn't say anything because if we did, they wouldn't let us leave."
>
> *Rosario Argilagos Rodríguez,*
> *who left Cuba at age fifty*

Emigration Slows

The end of the Freedom Flights slowed Cuban emigration to the United States considerably. From early 1973 to late 1979, only thirty-eight thousand Cubans came. Once again, Cubans who wanted to make the trip had to go first to another country or emigrate illegally by boat.

During 1979, a small number of Cubans sought refuge in the embassies of several South American nations, hoping that the foreign officials would help them leave Cuba. On March 28, 1980, a group of Cubans drove a truck through the gates of Peru's embassy in Havana. Within days, nearly eleven thousand Cubans who hoped to leave the country filled the embassy grounds. The United States and several other nations agreed to accept these people. On April 20, 1980, Castro announced that anyone with family in the United States who wanted to leave Cuba could do so.

The Mariel Boatlift

Americans in Florida quickly flocked to Cuba in boats. They anchored in the port of Mariel, Cuba, picked up passengers, and returned to Florida. The Mariel Boatlift, as it was known, lasted for a period of several months in 1980. By September of that year, about 125,000 people had left Cuba in the boatlift.

As the boatlift continued, it grew more controversial. Castro insisted that the Americans take anyone the Cuban authorities gave them as well as the people they had come to get. He forced some boats to take people from Cuban prisons and mental institutions. These people formed only a fraction of all those leaving Cuba, and many of the "criminals" had been jailed for buying food illegally or for their religious beliefs, not for any real crimes. Still, stories of criminals and mental patients—along with the problems caused by the arrival of large numbers of people at once—prompted the U.S. government to limit the boatlift. It put in place new rules that cut the number of people arriving. Finally, in late September 1980, Castro closed the port of Mariel, ending the boatlift.

▲ In 1980, the *Americana*, a fishing boat, crossed the Florida Straits during the Mariel Boatlift, packed with refugees. The little boat being pulled by the larger vessel was also carrying refugees.

A New U.S. Policy

In the decade after the boatlift, Cubans continued to emigrate. In 1984, the United States and Cuba agreed to allow twenty thousand Cubans to emigrate from Cuba to the United States each year. Between 1981 and 1990, nearly 145,000 people made the journey.

From 1990 to 1994, several thousand Cubans crossed the Florida Straits on boats and makeshift rafts. American and Cuban officials finally worked out an agreement in 1994. People with close family members already in the United States would be allowed to enter the country. Again, the United States agreed

"As part of its campaign against Cuba, the United States government authorized the illegal immigration of 3,500 people into its territory. In view of this, the Cuban government opened the port of Mariel for emigration. As a result more than 100,000 worthless individuals left the country."

Description of the Mariel Boatlift in Cuban History, *published in the 1990s and used in Cuban schools as a textbook for ninth graders*

to accept up to twenty thousand additional Cubans each year. The demand to leave Cuba is much greater than the slots available, however. For this reason, the visas needed to emigrate are handed out by lottery. Hundreds of thousands of people have registered for the few thousand lottery slots.

This agreement, like many others between the United States and Cuba, has not fared well. The United States has accused Cuba of blocking the departure of large numbers of people—fewer than

Elián González

In 1999, a tragic situation arose that involved a Cuban child named Elián González. The six-year-old boy was being taken by his mother on a raft across the Florida Straits late in 1999. When the raft tipped over, Elián's mother and ten other people drowned. Only the boy survived. After Elián was rescued, a great-uncle in Florida took him in, and his extended family hoped to raise him. The father, still in Cuba, claimed his son. (Elián's father and mother had divorced some years earlier.) The case soon became a public battle. Most non-Cuban Americans believed that the boy's father had the right to take him back to Cuba if that was what he wanted. Some thought that after the trauma of losing his mother, the boy should experience the healing that would come from living with his father.

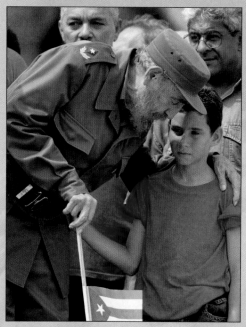

In 2000, Elián González was returned to Cuba from the United States. He was photographed at the 2005 May Day celebrations with President Fidel Castro.

Cuban Americans, however, pointed out that the Cuban government would eventually remove him from his family's home—as it did with all children in their teens—and place him in a special boarding school. They acknowledged the pain that arises from a child being separated from his parents—a pain many of them had experienced—but insisted that the opportunity to live freely in the United States made that pain worthwhile. A parent who really loved his child, they believed, would never deny that child such an opportunity. The U.S. government, however, sent Elián back to Cuba.

twenty thousand new immigrants actually arrive in the United States each year. The two nations have remained locked in disagreement on the issue.

Dry Foots

Every year, some Cubans decide to emigrate illegally, without a visa, most of them leaving by boat. In 1995, the United States introduced a policy called "wet foot/dry foot." Under this policy, Cubans who reach land are accepted into the United States. Any Cubans seized in the water, however, are returned to Cuba. The U.S. government also increased Coast Guard patrols of the Florida Straits.

Despite the dangers, many Cubans continue to risk the crossing. Unfortunately, some die at sea. Those who manage to reach U.S. shores are allowed to enter and are welcomed by Cuban Americans. In 2004, about 950 people arrived in the United States this way. In 2005, the number of "dry foots" was more than 2,500.

▼ Cubans picked up by the U.S. Coast Guard are held on board a vessel while their fates are decided. Under the United States' "wet foot/dry foot" policy, they are supposed to be returned to Cuba.

CHAPTER 3

Arriving in the United States

The number of Cubans who arrived in the United States before Fidel Castro came to power was small compared to the large numbers of Cubans who arrived later. These early arrivals from Cuba had little effect on U.S. society compared to immigrant groups from other nations, who came in much larger numbers during the same period.

The Early Arrivals

In the 1800s, most Cuban immigrants settled in Florida, while a smaller number made their way to New York City and northern New Jersey. After 1885, the majority went to Ybor City, Florida, where Cuban-owned cigar factories offering work had opened.

Immigrants arriving in the United States before 1875 could enter the country with few or no restrictions. After that date, various immigration laws began to control the flow of people seeking a new home in the United States. Through the 1950s, most Cubans were still allowed in, and they acquired the status

▼ At Miami International Airport in 1961, a crowd of anxious Cuban refugees wait to be processed—the first step to starting a new life in a foreign land.

> "When we finally walked off the plane, many people knelt and kissed the foreign soil with gratitude. I couldn't bring myself to do anything like that. I decided to save such a moment for a more private occasion, or perhaps for that faraway day when I returned to Cuba."
>
> *Cuban American Flor Fernandez Barrios, on arriving in the United States in 1970*

of resident aliens. After a certain number of years, Cubans could go through the process of naturalization and become U.S. citizens.

Refugee Status

In 1960, after Castro took power, the U.S. government gave Cuban refugees special "parole" status. Although they were not legally permanent residents, Cubans with parole status would be allowed to seek employment.

Cuban immigrants after 1959 had a significant impact on U.S. society and immigration policy. One reason is their much larger numbers—nearly nine hundred thousand of them. Another is the fact that many of these immigrants settled mainly in Florida, which raised issues about how they could be absorbed into the state's existing society and how Florida's economy could handle them.

When the exodus began, the United States was happy to accept Cuban refugees. U.S. officials felt it was the humanitarian thing to do, and it helped call attention to the failings of communism. The influx of Cubans caused tension in Miami, however, where people wondered if their community could cope with so many refugees.

A Helping Hand

To help solve the problem, the U.S. government set up the Cuban Refugee Emergency Center in downtown Miami. The center processed the new arrivals and encouraged some to resettle in other areas. Private aid groups, including churches, provided food and clothing. The U.S. government paid the cost of resettling families.

President John F. Kennedy took aid efforts further. His administration gave Cuban Americans funds for job training, health care, and schooling as well as resettlement. These larger aid efforts, and the growing number of Cubans in the Miami area, led to resentment against Cuban Americans among other residents of South Florida. Growing complaints convinced the government to push harder to resettle Cuban Americans in other states. By June 1963,

"They were a wonder-ful family. . . . They bought us coats; they really treated us as if we were their own children, like part of the family. . . . We were like equals. I cannot tell you that they treated their own children better than they did us."

Aurora Candelaria, who came with the Pedro Pan program in the 1960s and lived with a U.S. foster family until her parents arrived

about one-third of Cuban Americans had agreed to leave the Miami area.

The Pedro Pans

More than fourteen thousand Pedro Pan children had a different experience. They were met on arrival by workers from the Catholic Welfare Bureau or similar groups for Protestant and Jewish children. These groups placed the children in homes. Some Pedro Pan children went to live with members of their extended families, while others lived in group homes. Yet others were placed with American foster families.

Some of the Pedro Pan children were unhappy in their new homes, but others developed strong bonds with the families that took them in. All looked forward to the day they would be reunited with their own parents, which happened eventually for the majority of the children.

The Marielitos Arrive

When the "Marielitos" came in the 1980 Mariel Boatlift, the government set up processing centers at Key West and in the Miami area. Workers checked the papers of new arrivals, had them photographed and fingerprinted, and gave them medical exams. The immigrants had to answer many questions about their lives in Cuba, their job skills, and their political views. People with families in the United

▼ During the Mariel Boatlift of 1980, Cuban Americans wait on the dock at Key West, Florida, watching arriving boats for relatives and friends coming to the United States.

▲ For some Marielitos, there was nowhere to go when they arrived in the United States. This airplane hangar in Key West became a temporary home for many of them.

States were processed fairly quickly. Those with no family connections were held longer, sometimes in government-built tent cities.

Cuban Americans greeted the Mariel refugees warmly at first—many, after all, were family members. When news got out that some of the Marielitos were criminals or people with mental health problems, attitudes toward them soured.

As more and more Marielitos arrived, the government had to open more processing centers, including three outside Florida. With no families to claim them, these Cubans had to spend months in the camps. Conditions worsened, as did the mood of the new arrivals. In the summer of 1980, riots broke out at three camps. The violence added to the negative view of Marielitos. Over time, however, the majority of Marielitos found homes and jobs. Some were resettled in other states, but the majority remained in Florida.

The Cuban Adjustment Act

Cubans admitted on a "parole" status could not become permanent residents, and that meant they could not become citizens. In 1966, however, Congress passed the Cuban Adjustment Act, which allowed parolees to apply for legal residency and, later, go through naturalization. Cubans seized that opportunity. From 1966 to 1975, more than 136,000 Cuban Americans became U.S. citizens, the largest group of immigrants from any foreign nation to do so in this period. Many Cuban Americans still choose to become U.S. citizens today.

CHAPTER 4

The First Community

Cubans who came to the United States in the late 1800s and early 1900s established the foundation of Cuban American life. These early arrivals set up communities that attracted later arrivals from Cuba.

The political exiles were almost all white, and many came from the landowning class. They always kept their eyes set on Cuba and established their own communities apart from U.S. society. The immigrants who came seeking work were mainly interested in making a living, although they also kept in touch with developments in Cuba. These workers included a large number of black Cubans.

▼ Vincente Ybor built small houses in Ybor City, Florida, and rented them to workers in the cigar industry. Not until the 1920s did the workers' houses get indoor plumbing or electrical power.

The Cigar Makers

The first major Cuban community in the United States was in Key West, Florida—the point closest to Cuba. A few Cubans in the business of making cigars moved operations to Key West from Cuba in the late 1800s. One of them, Vincente Martínez Ybor, soon decided that Key West was not the location he wanted. He bought some open land near Tampa, Florida, and used it to construct a whole new town.

Ybor City, founded in 1885, became the center of the Cuban American community. The new city had little to offer at first. José Vega Diaz arrived in 1892 and recalled that the area had "no light [and] no electric." Eventually, the town had electric trolleys that people could take to work. There were stores, restaurants, and churches as well.

Dozens of cigar factories sprang up in Ybor City—some large, like Ybor's own, and some smaller. The cigar industry employed several thousand people, and Ybor City was seen as the cigar capital of the world.

▲ A lector on a raised platform reads to workers in this 1929 photograph of the Cuesta-Ray cigar factory in Ybor City.

The Lector

Each Ybor City cigar factory had a special worker called the *lector*, or reader, a tradition brought from Cuba. While workers cut tobacco and rolled cigars, the lector read to them. The lectors were hired for the quality of their voices and expression. In the mornings, they read from newspapers and magazines. In the afternoons, they read novels, poetry, and histories. The workers chipped in part of their wages to pay the lectors, who were highly regarded. In the early 1930s, factory owners began to bar lectors because they read news about the forming of labor unions. In 1931, cigar factory workers staged a strike to bring the readers back, but the factory owners won the battle, and the lectors were gone.

Facing Segregation

Black Cubans who came to the city found themselves living under southern segregation laws. When

▲ Cuban Americans in Florida were active in the independence movement. They formed a political group called the Cuban Revolutionary Society in this building in Key West, Florida.

"First, we were driven here by political troubles, but when the independence of Cuba was proclaimed many left [the United States] immediately. I was one of the first to go, leaving the next day with my wife. At first I liked to sit under a royal palm enjoying the fresh air with my wife and children, but it takes something besides air on which to live. We have to eat, so I came back to Tampa [to work] and am here yet."

Rodolfo Blain, speech to Cuban Americans in Tampa, 1907

they left Ybor City to go to nearby Tampa, they had to use black-only facilities. Racial differences had been present in Cuba, too, and these carried over to the U.S. In the cigar factories, blacks and whites worked together, but social and political groups formed by Cuban Americans were split by race. This was true even after José Martí came to Ybor City in 1891 and urged Cubans to bury their racial differences and work together for an independent Cuba based on equality.

Although they had separate groups, workers of both races did show their dedication to the cause of independence. Many took part in what was called *El Día de la Patria* (the Day of the Homeland) in which they donated one day's pay each week to the independence movement.

Life in the Early 1900s

Ybor City thrived for several decades, and Cuban Americans dominated the city. Even after Cuba's independence, most Cuban Americans remained in Ybor City, where life was relatively easy and there was work available. Since the community was thoroughly Cuban, many felt at home. With Cuba only a short distance away, they could visit family when they wanted to.

After Cuba won independence, the cigar workers focused on winning rights for themselves. They began to form labor unions and push for better pay and better hours. Factory owners struck back by buying machinery that took the place of workers. Economic conditions hit the workers as well. The Great Depression that began in 1929 forced owners to close factories and pushed workers out of jobs. The growing popularity of cigarettes also hurt the cigar industry. By the 1940s, Ybor City's cigar industry was only a memory.

Cuban immigrants built other communities in Florida: in Miami, Jacksonville, Key West, and Pensacola. Cuban American neighborhoods also appeared in New York City and cities in northern New Jersey, such as Union City. These communities tended to be small, and members had to work within U.S. society. They could not enjoy a mainly Cuban culture, as in Ybor City. Still, they set up *bodegas* and other businesses, which formed the foundation of communities that would be joined by many more Cuban Americans in the 1960s.

Cuban Music and Entertainers

Some Cuban American entertainers gained fame in the middle 1900s. Americans who visited Cuba liked its music, and Cuban musicians traveled to the United States to take advantage of that popularity. The first was a bandleader named Xavier Cugat, who started performing in the 1930s. He was followed by a percussionist named Desi Arnaz, whose family fled to the United States for political reasons. In the 1940s, Arnaz popularized a dance called the conga, in which people danced in a long line. Arnaz moved to Hollywood and made a couple of movies. There, he met and married comedienne Lucille Ball. Together, they launched a television show called *I Love Lucy* that became one of the most popular shows of all time. In the mid-1950s, about fifty million people watched the show each week.

A magazine cover from 1956 features Desi Arnaz and his family.

CHAPTER 5

Living in Exile

The vast majority of the post-Castro exiles were from the middle class or, later, the working class. Having given up everything they owned when they left Cuba, they had to rely on hard work and their personal abilities to build new lives for themselves. Cuban Americans also drew on the help of family and friends and, to some extent, help from the government and private charities. Starting from little or nothing, they built a thriving and successful Cuban American community.

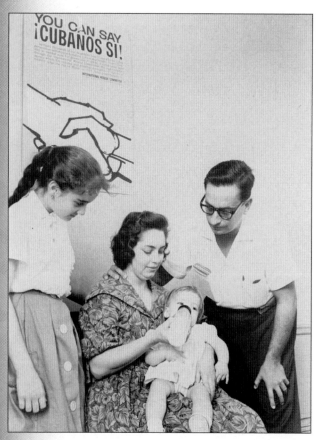

Cuban American Settlement

Efforts to resettle the exiles who came in the 1960s succeeded to a degree. By 1972, more than 270,000 Cubans had been placed all over the country. Some states had more than others: New York had 80,000, while Alaska was home to a single Cuban American.

Most exiles who came in the 1960s, however, settled

◀ A refugee family waits in the office of the International Rescue Committee in New York City in 1961. Cuban American communities formed in New York and New Jersey during the 1960s and 1970s.

▲ Miami's Little Havana, with Calle Ocho (Eighth Street) at its heart, is still the center of the Cuban American community today. During the annual Calle Ocho festival, shown here in 2005, crowds enjoy music, dancing, and Cuban American food.

in South Florida. By 1970, nearly half of all Cuban Americans lived in that area. New York City had another 16 percent, and northern New Jersey had just less than 13 percent. In New Jersey, Cubans clustered in communities north of Jersey City, such as Hoboken, Union City, North Bergen, and West New York. Fewer than 10 percent of Cuban Americans lived in California.

In Miami, an area west of downtown came to be called "Little Havana." New banks, restaurants, shops, and other Cuban or Latino businesses sprang up along Eighth Street. The center of Little Havana, this street became known as *Calle Ocho* (Eighth Street in Spanish).

Finding Work

As with other immigrant groups, Cuban Americans found they had to start at the bottom of the economic ladder, even if they arrived with skills. Cuban immigrant

> "My father started working at the Americana Hotel in Miami. His job was to help the busboy. He used to work mostly nights. . . . My father was very proud. . . . But he wasn't too proud that he couldn't do this menial job just to get food on the table. . . . He was willing to go around picking up dirty dishes, and taking them down to be washed."
>
> *Ramon Fernandez, who came to Miami from Cuba in 1961*

Carlos Arboleya had been a top financial officer in Cuba's largest bank. When he reached Miami, however, he was unable to get a job in a bank. Arboleya began working in a shoe factory. In less than two years, he was a vice president of the shoe company. A few years later, Arboleya reentered banking and eventually became president of one of Miami's largest banks.

Many wives worked outside the home—far more than in other Latino groups. One reason was Cubans' strong work ethic. Another

A Cuban American Family

Born in 1910, twelfth in a family of thirteen, David Padrino became a doctor in Cuba. He married his wife Ilda in 1945, and they had two sons and a daughter. Because of his profession, Padrino was not allowed to emigrate when Castro came to power, but in 1962 the Padrinos sent their children

to the United States as part of Operation Pedro Pan. The children went to live with an uncle who had settled in New York in the 1930s. Five years later, the Padrinos were finally able to join their children. Although in his late fifties, Padrino went through the rigorous process of gaining certification to practice medicine in the United States. He settled in New York, where he worked in several hospitals and as a company doctor, as well as running a private practice. Padrino's work enabled him to fund his children's education.

The Padrinos spoke Spanish at home, listened to Cuban music, and cooked and ate Cuban food, although they also enjoyed U.S. traditions, such as the Fourth of July. The Padrino children carried on the family work ethic, studying to become a doctor, a lawyer, and a teacher. None of the three married a Cuban American, but all made sure that their own children learned Spanish.

▲ (*Top*) This photo shows Dr. David Padrino after gaining his U.S. medical certification. (*Bottom*) The Padrinos, shown here in the 1970s, were reunited with their Pedro Pan children in 1967.

was the need for a second income in order to survive in their new homes. In addition, many Cuban families included three generations, so grandparents could watch children while mothers worked.

Professionals found it difficult to pick up their old careers, but the U.S. government set up programs to help doctors and teachers gain the training and language skills they needed. Lawyers had the most difficulty renewing their careers because the legal system in the United States was completely different from the one in Cuba.

Spanish and English

Cuban American children learned English in school. In the early 1960s, the Dade County school system, which includes Miami, put in place a bilingual education program. It called for teachers to instruct students in subject areas using Spanish while, in other classes, the students learned English. In this way, they could remain at the appropriate grade level in math, science, and social studies while gaining English skills.

Many adults who lived in primarily Cuban American communities spoke only Spanish, while adults who worked outside those areas learned English. Cuban parents often relied on their children for help by having them translate when visiting non-Spanish-speaking areas.

Family Life

Cuban Americans had a deep commitment to the family, and the nuclear family was a vital structure for them. Cuban American children tended not to challenge their parents openly. Within the home, children showed respect and deferred to their parents' wishes.

Many Cuban American men became less authoritarian when wives working outside the home

"Not speaking English was a barrier for both my parents. At first, they were taken with the idea of going to school in the evenings, but soon they realized they were too tired at night to learn anything. So my brother and I became the designated interpreters. . . . Being older and female, I was forced by circumstance to go everywhere with my parents—to doctors, the dentist, to stores and any other place where English was required."

Flor Fernandez Barrios, recalling life in California in the early 1970s

demanded greater equality. Those demands, however, did not always produce a smooth family life. The rate of divorce among Cuban Americans rose over the years. In 1980, only 5.2 percent of Cuban Americans were divorced. Ten years later, 8.3 percent were divorced. Nearly half the Cuban American women who grew up in the United States married non-Cubans—far more than other Latino American women who married outside their groups.

Grandparents often lived with their children and grandchildren, and many young adults continued to live in their parents' homes until they married. Older children were expected to focus on their studies rather than work outside the home. But some practices had to be abandoned in the face of new realities. The practice of chaperoning young women on dates, for example, was largely dropped. Young Cuban Americans, seeing the freedom enjoyed by non-Cuban Americans of their age, would not accept chaperones. On the other hand, Cuban American girls typically had earlier curfews than males of the same age.

Maintaining Tradition

Cuban Americans kept, but adapted, some traditions from Cuba. The traditional Sunday meal that included the extended family was maintained if possible. If the family lived too far apart or if new lifestyles required work on Sunday, it was dropped. Cuban Americans continued the practice of giving their daughters a *quinceañera* party on their fifteenth birthday. Some parents, however, turned the parties into expensive events unlike those seen in Cuba.

In the early 1970s, Castro banned celebration of Three Kings' Day in Cuba. Cuban Americans in South Florida, however, began staging a Three Kings' Day Parade that became an annual event. Another religious tradition involves la Virgen de la Caridad del Cobre (Our Lady of Charity)—the patron

"The most important thing was to reunite the family. . . . When we came to this very welcoming country, we immediately reunited with the children, and this was the greatest wish of all Cubans, to bring the family back together and live together and maintain all their patriotic and democratic ideals."

Ilda Arbelo, who came to the United States in 1967 after five years' separation from her children

▲ Many Cuban Americans worship at the Ermita de la Caridad, the Miami shrine built by Cuban Americans in 1973 to house the statue of la Virgen de la Caridad del Cobre. The shrine faces seaward toward Cuba.

saint of Cuba. People pray to her when they are troubled or need help. Funded by donations, a shrine was built in Miami to hold a statue of the Virgen that had been brought from Cuba in 1961.

Forming Organizations

Cuban Americans formed various kinds of organizations. Some were Cuban groups transplanted to the United States, but others were newly formed. Among the first groups founded in the 1960s were *municipios*. People who came from the same municipio (township) in Cuba joined together in the United States to form a group that was a kind of mutual aid society. The groups kept lists of everyone from the town living in exile so that people could easily contact old friends. They provided job and housing information and raised money to be sent back to families in Cuba.

Cultural groups included companies that performed *zarzuelas*, or popular operas; others put on plays or played traditional music. Former editors once again produced books, some that explored Cuban history and culture and others that analyzed the current situation on the island. Groups with different political ideas published their own newspapers.

El Nuevo Herald

In 1976, the Miami *Herald* began publishing a version of the newspaper, called *El Herald*, a Spanish translation of the stories in the English-language paper. The paper was aimed at the growing community of Cuban Americans and other Spanish speakers in the area. Circulation did grow, but not as much as the publishers had hoped. In 1987, the publisher revamped the Spanish newspaper, changing its name to *El Nuevo Herald* (The New Herald) and creating a completely separate reporting and editorial staff. Within three years, the new paper's circulation topped 100,000. *El Nuevo Herald* has won several journalism awards.

Political Activity

Among the political groups that formed, many shared a common goal—promoting the day Castro would be gone from Cuba. Some groups gathered weapons and made plans to attack the island. Others made contact with dissidents on the island in the hope of helping them change the regime.

Some political groups were extreme. They carried out terrorist actions against those who disagreed with them or who supported Fidel Castro. Over time, these practices mostly died out, but they did occasionally recur. In the late 1980s, a Cuban American art museum held an exhibit of Cuban works, including some by artists who supported Castro. Unidentified people exploded a bomb outside the museum.

Other Cuban Americans focused on actions that influenced U.S. government policy toward Cuba. In the 1980s and 1990s, they also supported the U.S. government in setting up radio and television stations, called Radio Martí and TV Martí, that broadcast Spanish-language programming to Cuba. Some Cuban Americans took advantage of the radio station to send personal messages to family members on the island. Castro's government often jammed the signals of these stations.

Success and Poverty

Many exiles who came in the 1960s achieved tremendous success. Their education and training in Cuba; their drive and desire to succeed; and the initial boost provided by family, friends, and government aid all helped produce these results. By 1980, nearly half of the Cuban Americans who lived in Dade County, Florida, worked as professionals, business owners, managers, or in other high-level jobs. Three out of every five Cuban Americans owned a home.

▶ Several monuments in Cuban American communities are dedicated to the struggles of the Cuban people during the last one hundred years. This monument in Miami honors those who took part in the failed Bay of Pigs invasion in 1961.

Everyone did not share in this success, however. Many Cuban Americans were poor and endured crowded housing, bad nutrition, ill health, and little education. Black Cuban Americans in particular faced problems. They earned far less than white Cuban Americans and suffered more from unemployment. Some poorer Cuban Americans worked in businesses owned by other Cuban Americans where they felt overworked and underpaid, causing friction within the community.

Bitterness and Hope

Although the exiles who came in the 1960s gained freedom and success, their experience was laced with sadness, nostalgia, bitterness, and hope. It was painful for Cuban Americans to leave behind the island they loved and face the possibility that they could never return. Feeding their sadness was nostalgia for *la Cuba de ayer* (the Cuba of yesterday). Photos, records, videos, and cassettes allowed them to relive the sights and sounds of their lost homeland. Enjoying those mem-

The Cuban American National Foundation

The Cuban American National Foundation (CANF), founded in 1981, is the largest and most influential Cuban American group. Fiercely opposed to Fidel Castro, it does many different kinds of work. CANF regularly publishes accounts of the suppression of human rights in Cuba and takes other actions to criticize Castro's government. CANF gained influence in U.S. state and national politics as the importance of the Cuban American vote grew. Since the 1997 death of its founder, Jorge Más Canosa, the group has lost some of its influence in the United States.

▲ Older Cuban Americans often meet over coffee and dominoes to discuss politics. These players were photographed in Domino Park in Miami's Little Havana.

ories produced sadness and bitter anger focused on Castro. Hope remained, however. At Christmas, many Cuban Americans toasted each other by saying, "Next year, in Cuba."

Among many older Cuban Americans, those attitudes remained for many years. By the 1970s, those who arrived at a younger age—and some older people as well—focused more on their new lives in the United States.

Attitudes toward the Marielitos

The Marielitos, who came in 1980, were different from the exiles of the 1960s. The adults were younger by an average of ten years; there were more blacks and people of mixed race; and they were mostly working class, single men rather than middle-class families.

Marielitos were not always welcomed by Cuban Americans already in the United States. One reason was the bad reputation they unfairly received from news stories. Older exiles had another concern as well. The Marielitos had lived twenty years in communist Cuba. Many had been educated in its schools and served in its army. Cuban Americans who had come much earlier worried that the Marielitos would have different values and viewpoints than their own.

The Marielito Experience

The Marielitos closely followed the patterns of the earlier arrivals. The vast majority—nearly three of every four—settled in Florida. Other common destinations were New York, New Jersey, California, and Illinois, which all had existing Cuban American communities. The new immigrants found work and worked hard. Unemployment among them was high at first, but by 1990 it had dropped to just over 5 percent, close to the national average. Many embraced the chance to get ahead by taking on responsibility. By the late 1980s, nearly one-quarter of Marielitos owned their own businesses.

Children of the Mariel Boatlift learned English quickly. By the late 1980s, less than 10 percent needed bilingual education programs. They succeeded in school, and about the same proportion of Marielito children went to college as did earlier Cuban Americans.

Recent Arrivals

More recent arrivals from Cuba have followed similar patterns. People came in smaller numbers, and they have more easily entered the Cuban American community. The hardships faced in Cuba since the early 1990s have convinced many professionals, yet again, to leave the country. Some of these people, like those in earlier groups, have had to repeat their training in order to resume their careers in the United States.

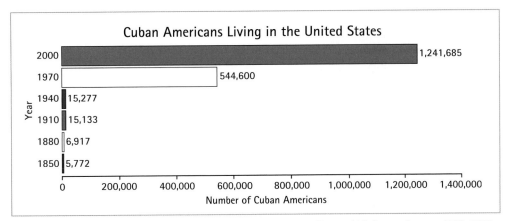

Source: U.S. Census Bureau, 1850–2000

▲ The Cuban American population jumped from about 540,000 to more than 800,000 in 1980, when the Marielitos arrived, and to over 1 million by 2000.

Cuban
Americans
in U.S. Society

Today, between 1.2 and 1.5 million Cuban Americans live in the United States. They are the country's third largest Latino group, after Mexican Americans (more than 25 million) and Puerto Ricans (about 4 million). The vast majority of Cuban Americans live in cities, and three-fourths of all Cubans live in or near Miami, New York City, or Los Angeles, California.

Most Cuban Americans were born in Cuba. According to the 2000 U.S. census, their average age was nearly forty-one years, which is six years older than the average for the whole U.S. population. The age of Cuban Americans is much higher than that of other Latino groups. These figures probably reflect the fact that Cuban American families tend to have fewer children.

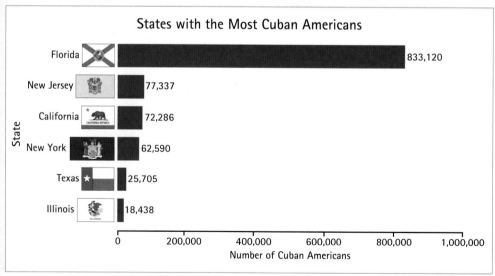

Source: U.S. Census Bureau, Census 2000

▲ This chart shows where most Cuban Americans live today. The vast majority still live in Florida, but there are Cuban Americans and Cuban American communities in other states, too.

About 25 percent of Cuban Americans age twenty-five and older have a college degree, compared to only 7 percent of Mexican Americans and 13 percent of Puerto Ricans in the United States. The figure for Cuban Americans, however, is slightly lower than that of non-Latino whites in the country. The average income of Cuban American families is about the same as that for non-Latino whites and is higher than other American Latino groups. The average income of Cuban American women is higher than other groups of Latino women. Nearly three out of five Cuban Americans own their own homes—also a higher rate than among other Latinos.

In and Around Miami

The overwhelming share of Cuban Americans—two out of every three—live in Florida. More than half of the total population live in Dade County, which includes Miami. As more Cuban Americans settled in the area, they spread beyond the city of Miami to nearby towns such as Hialeah, Sweetwater, and Coral Gables. Miami's Little Havana, however, remains the heart of the Cuban American community. There, Cuban Americans celebrate their *cubanidad* (Cubanness) with memorials honoring Cuba and Cuban heroes, by playing dominoes, or by arguing about politics and baseball while enjoying Cuban coffee.

Tension exists between Cuban Americans and other Miami-area groups. Members of other Latino groups sometimes resent Cuban American domination of politics and culture there, and some African

▶ Stores in Cuban American communities offer many Latino goods. The Casa de las Piñatas, a Cuban American business in Miami's Little Havana, sells piñatas for all occasions.

Americans and Haitians in South Florida are still bitter about the assistance the U.S. government gave Cuban immigrants.

Other Communities

Sizable Cuban American communities exist in New York City, northern New Jersey, and a few other areas. There, bodegas sell Cuban food, and other features of Cuban American life are evident.

Some Cuban Americans live in different parts of the country for professional or personal reasons. With no larger community to join, they typically blend into mainstream U.S. culture. Visits to family and friends in Miami, looking at Cuban American web sites, and ordering Cuban food by mail help them maintain their cubanidad.

"Only those immigrants who arrived here between infancy and adulthood share both the [Cubanness] of their parents and the Americanness of their children. . . . My parents, who are now in their early seventies, have no choice but to be Cuban. No matter how many years they have resided away from the island . . . they are as Cuban today as they were when they got off the ferry in October 1960. My children, who were born in this country of Cuban parents . . . are American through and through. . . . Like other second-generation immigrants, they maintain a connection to their parents' homeland, but it is a bond forged by my experiences rather than their own."

Cuban American Gustavo Pérez-Firmat, 1994

Speaking Spanish

Spanish remains a vital part of Cuban Americans' lives. About 70 percent of Cuban Americans speak Spanish in social situations. In South Florida, up to half speak Spanish at work. Those who arrived as children in the early and mid-1900s knew that learning English would help them get ahead, however, and many became bilingual. When they get together with other Cuban Americans, they frequently switch between the two languages. Cuban Americans have contributed to the growth of what is called "Spanglish," the making of new Spanish words out of English ones.

Division Among Generations

The majority of Cuban Americans agree on several things. They agree that Cuba would be better off without Castro and that democracy and human rights in Cuba should be supported. They also share deep pride in Cuban culture and the achievements of Cuban Americans. Some differences divide the Cuban American community, however.

Divisions often arise from generational differences. Those Cuban Americans who were children when they came in the 1960s and 1970s have grown up in the United States. Their memories of Cuba are distant, and they have embraced U.S. culture. They are more skeptical about the role of Cuban Americans in shaping Cuba's future. Children of this younger generation—many born into marriages between Cubans and non-Cubans—are even more American.

▲ Cultural traditions from Cuba, such as art forms derived from the Orisha religion, are maintained by Cuban Americans. Neri Torres, performing here at the Historical Museum of Southern Florida, uses Orisha traditions in her dance performances.

These differences do not always sit well with the older generation. One older Cuban American remarked, "Despite all our efforts, our children are more American than Cuban. Their lives are different from mine. Sometimes I don't understand them at all. . . . And *their* children don't speak Spanish at all. It's a shame."

Cuban Heritage
In spite of the differences between generations, Cuban Americans—like many other groups in the United States—keep their heritage alive. Many Cuban American families still enjoy the traditional Christmas Eve dinner of roast pork, black beans, rice, and yuca, and many also share *arroz con pollo* (chicken and rice) as a family meal on Sundays. They still enjoy watching baseball and playing dominoes, and they have helped fuel the popularity of Spanish-language television. Cuban American men, especially in South Florida, can often be spotted from the shirts they wear. Called *guayaberas,* these shirts are made of cool cotton or linen and include several pleats. Older Cuban Americans listen to the songs they heard on the island in their youth. Many who came at

▲ A baker makes traditional Cuban pastries at the Cafe Cubano in Little Havana.

Cuban American Food

Cuban food has gained wide popularity across the United States. Cuban dishes, such as roast pork, black beans and rice, and Cuban sandwiches are served not only in South Florida, but in many cities across the country. In Little Havana and elsewhere, stores sell Cuban varieties of potatoes, such as *malanga* and *boniato*, and other ingredients used in the vegetable stew *ajiaco*. Cuban cooking has also become part of the popular fusion cuisine, which blends foods from different cultures.

younger ages enjoy these songs as well. Willy Chirino, once a Pedro Pan child, has issued a CD of traditional Cuban music.

Cuban American Influence

Some of this heritage has had an impact on mainstream culture in the United States. Cuban band music was wildly popular from the 1930s to the 1960s. In more recent years, singers, including Gloria Estefan and Jon Secada, won popularity with non-Latino audiences as well as Latinos. Cristina Saralegui hosted a daytime television talk show that was so popular among Latinos that she was compared to Oprah Winfrey. Novelists Oscar Hijuelos and Cristina García have written award-winning novels. In recent years, several people have written moving accounts of their lives in Cuba and their transition to life in the United States. These books not only reveal Cuban culture and ideas but also explore how people form their identities and what it means to be American.

Cuban Americans in the Economy and Government

One of the most significant contributions of Cuban Americans to U.S. society has been in the growth of the economy and community in South Florida. In 1960, Dade County had a population of fewer than one million people. Today, the population has more than doubled to well over two million. By 2000, it was the eighth largest county in the United States. It has become the world's fifth largest center of the telecommunications industry, the base for more than five hundred companies that do business around the world, an international banking center, and the gateway to U.S. trade with Latin America. While this growth is not solely the work of Cuban Americans, they have played a vital role in it.

The Cuban American community in South Florida has gained considerable political power. Three Cuban Americans, Ileana Ros-Lehtinen and brothers Lincoln and Mario Diaz-Balart, have served in the U.S. House of Representatives for some years. In 2005, Mel Martinez, who came to the United States in the Pedro Pan program, became a U.S. senator from Florida. Some people say that Cuban Americans have dominated U.S. foreign policy toward Cuba, and that this policy has not been successful.

Struggling and Succeeding

Many Cuban immigrants suffered—and still do suffer—from discrimination in the United States. Some have endured verbal insults and questions about their intelligence because they did not speak English well. But although many have struggled, Cuban Americans have never developed the idea that they were a minority population being held down by other groups of Americans.

Keeping alive Cuban music, food, and culture helps Cuban Americans maintain their identity. That identity—their cubanidad—is very strong, and it helps them live successfully in a new land.

▼ In 2005, an exhibition at the Smithsonian's National Museum of American History featured the life and music of Celia Cruz. A celebrated singer who died in 2003, Cruz helped bring Cuban music into the mainstream of U.S. society. In this photograph, Cruz' husband Pedro Knight looks at a photo of himself with his wife.

Notable Cuban Americans

Desi Arnaz (1917–1986) Cuban-born bandleader and television star who popularized the conga and starred in the long-running sitcom *I Love Lucy* with his wife Lucille Ball.

Celia Cruz (1924–2003) Cuban-born singer who became a major star in the 1950s and moved to the United States in the 1960s, where she was known as the "Queen of Salsa" and was widely loved for her voice and spirit.

Roberto Goizueta (1932–1997) Cuban-born businessman who came to United States with his family after Castro came to power. In 1979, he became president of the Coca-Cola Company, which he led with great success.

Oscar Hijuelos (1951–) U.S.-born novelist from New York City whose second novel, *The Mambo Kings Play Songs of Love*, made him the first Latino to win a Pulitzer Prize for fiction.

José Martí (1853–1895) Cuban-born poet and leader in the struggle for Cuban independence, who was exiled from Cuba in his teens, lived in New York City for many years, and became a hero to Cubans and Cuban Americans when he died fighting for independence.

Mel Martinez (1946–) Cuban-born politician who came to the United States in Operation Pedro Pan. He served as mayor of Orange County, Florida, and secretary of Housing and Urban Development before becoming, in 2005, the first Cuban American to sit in the U.S. Senate.

Tony Pérez (1942–) Cuban-born baseball player who helped the Cincinnati Reds win two World Series in the 1970s and was elected to the Baseball Hall of Fame in 2000.

Ileana Ros-Lehtinen (1952–) Cuban-born politician who came to United States at age seven and, after working as a teacher, entered politics and won election to the Florida state legislature in 1982 and to the U.S. House in 1989.

Cristina Saralegui (1948–) Cuban-born print and television journalist who came to the United States in 1960. She worked as editor in chief of a Spanish-language version of *Cosmopolitan* magazine before hosting a highly popular Spanish-language television talk show.

Vincente Martinez Ybor (1818–1896) Spanish-born businessman who built Ybor City, which became the center of the world's cigar industry.

Time Line

1868 Ten Years' War begins in Cuba.

1885 Ybor City is founded in Florida.

1895 Cuban patriots declare new war to fight for Cuban independence.

1898 April 25: United States declares war on Spain, beginning Spanish-American War.

      December 24: Spain surrenders Cuba to U.S. control.

1901 Cuba writes its own constitution and forms a government.

1902 United States hands control of Cuba to its own republican government.

1952 Fulgencio Batista seizes control of Cuban government.

1958 December 31: Batista flees Cuba and Fidel Castro gains power in Cuba.

1959 May 17: Castro issues land reform decree.

1960 December 26: First Pedro Pan flight leaves from Cuba.

1961 January 3: United States cuts off diplomatic relations with Cuba.

      April 17: Bay of Pigs invasion begins.

1962 February 7: U.S. trade embargo blocks sale of goods to Cuba.

      October 22: Cuban Missile Crisis begins.

      October 28: Soviet leader Nikita Khrushchev agrees to take missiles out of Cuba, ending Cuban Missile Crisis.

1965 September 28: Castro announces that Cubans with family in the United States may emigrate.

      December 1: Freedom Flights begin.

1966 November 2: Congress passes Cuban Adjustment Act, allowing Cuban immigrants to become legal residents.

1973 April 6: Last of Freedom Flights lands in United States.

1980 March 28: Six Cubans crash a bus through the fence surrounding Peruvian embassy in Havana.

      April 20: Castro announces that anyone who wants to leave Cuba can do so, launching Mariel Boatlift.

      September 29: Last boat in Mariel Boatlift reaches Florida.

1984 U.S. and Cuba agree to allow 20,000 Cubans to immigrate to the United States each year.

1985 Radio Martí begins broadcasting from the United States to Cuba.

1987 *El Nuevo Herald* newspaper is launched in Miami.

1990 TV Martí begins broadcasting from the United States to Cuba.

1994 September 9: United States and Cuba agree on new immigration rules.

1995 U.S. and Cuba agree that refugees seized at sea will be returned to Cuba.

2000 Elián González is returned to Cuba after being rescued at sea in 1999.

2005 Mel Martinez becomes first Cuban American member of the U.S. Senate.

Glossary

alien person living in a nation other than his or her birth nation and who has not become a citizen of his or her new nation of residence

bilingual having to do with or able to speak two languages

bodega small Hispanic grocery store

census official population count

colony nation, territory, or people under the control of another country

communist political system in which government has strong control and property is shared among all citizens

culture language, beliefs, customs, and ways of life shared by a group of people from the same region or nation

discrimination treatment of one group or person differently from another

dissident person who voices disagreement with the policies of the government in his or her country

embargo law that blocks trade with another nation

emigrate leave one nation or region to go and live in another place

exile person who is forced or feels compelled to leave his or her homeland

exodus mass emigration of people from a particular region or nation

heritage something handed down from previous generations

immigrant person who arrives in a new nation or region to take up residence

labor union organization, often in a particular trade or business, that represents the rights of workers

Latino Spanish-speaking person from Latin America

mutual aid society organization in which members of the group, who are usually from a common background, help each other and perform social services separately from government agencies or private businesses

naturalization process of becoming a citizen by living in the United States for a number of years and passing a citizenship test

patron saint Catholic saints who are named as having special protective powers over a village, region, or aspect of life

prejudice bias against or dislike of a person or group because of race, nationality, or other factors

propaganda information, sometimes true and sometimes false, presented in a way that favors a particular point of view

ration limit the distribution of goods

refugee person who leaves a country or region because of conflict, natural disaster, or persecution

revolution sudden or fundamental change in the way things are done, often involving conflict

segregation separation of different ethnic or racial groups

strait narrow stretch of water between two bodies of land

Three Kings' Day Roman Catholic holiday on January 6 that celebrates the day the three Magi, or kings, gave their gifts to the newborn Jesus

visa document that permits a person to enter a nation for a set period of time

Further Resources

Books

Carey, Charles W. *Castro's Cuba*. History Firsthand (series). San Diego: Greenhaven Press, 2004.

Engfer, Lee. *Cubans in America*. In America (series). Minneapolis: Lerner Publications, 2005.

Gay, Kathlyn. *Leaving Cuba: From Operation Pedro Pan to Elian*. Minneapolis: Millbrook Press, 2000.

Hoobler, Dorothy and Thomas Hoobler. *The Cuban American Family Album*. New York: Oxford University Press, 1998.

Web Sites

Afro-Cuban Orisha Arts in Miami

www.historical-museum.org/exhibits/orisha/english/orisha-e-1.htm

Online Orisha exhbition from Historical Museum of Southern Florida

Introduction to the Cuban Heritage Collection

www.library.miami.edu/chc/chc.html

Images and words from the University of Miami about the experience of Cuban American exile

Publisher's note to educators and parents: Our editors have carefully reviewed these Web sites to ensure that they are suitable for children. Many Web sites change frequently, however, and we cannot guarantee that a site's future contents will continue to meet our high standards of quality and educational value. Be advised that children should be closely supervised whenever they access the Internet.

Where to Visit

Ybor City Museum State Park
1818 Ninth Avenue
Tampa, FL 33605
Telephone: (813) 247-6323
www.floridastateparks.org/Yborcity/default.cfm

About the Author

Dale Anderson studied history and literature at Harvard University in Cambridge, Massachusetts. He lives in Newtown, Pennsylvania, where he writes and edits educational books. Anderson has written many books for young people, including a history of Ellis Island, published by World Almanac® Library in its *Landmark Events in American History* series.

Index